SUPER SHEROES

OF SCIENCE

Advancing
Technology

Women Who Led the Way

SUPRIYA SAHAI

Children's Press®
An imprint of Scholastic Inc.

Library of Congress Cataloging-in-Publication Data
Names: Sahai, Supriya, 1977- author.
Title: Advancing technology : women who led the way / by Supriya Sahai.
Description: First edition. | New York, NY : Children's Press, an imprint of Scholastic Inc., 2022. |
   Series: Super SHEroes of science | Includes bibliographical references and index. | Audience: Ages 8-10. |
   Audience: Grades 4-6. | Summary: Audience: Ages 8-10. | Audience: Grades 4-6. | Summary: "This brand-new series
   highlights some of the major contributions women have made in the world of science. Photographs throughout"—
   Provided by publisher.
Identifiers: LCCN 2021037472 (print) | LCCN 2021037473 (ebook) | ISBN
   9781338800388 (library binding) | ISBN 9781338800395 (paperback) | ISBN 9781338800401 (ebk)
Subjects: LCSH: Women in technology—Biography—Juvenile literature. | Women scientists—Biography
   —Juvenile literature. | Technology—History—Juvenile literature. | BISAC: JUVENILE NONFICTION /
   Biography & Autobiography / Women
Classification: LCC T36 .S25 2022 (print) | LCC T36 (ebook) | DDC
   609.2/52—dc23
LC record available at https://lccn.loc.gov/2021037472
LC ebook record available at https://lccn.loc.gov/2021037473

Picture credits:

Photos ©: cover top: Children's Climate Prize; cover center top: NASA Image Collection/Alamy Images; cover center bottom: Adrian Cadiz/US Air Force/Wikimedia; cover bottom: Silver Screen Collection/Getty Images; 5 left: Children's Climate Prize; 5 center left: NASA Image Collection/Alamy Images; 5 center right: Adrian Cadiz/US Air Force/Wikimedia; 5 right: Silver Screen Collection/Getty Images; 6 inset top: Niday Picture Library/Alamy Images; 8 top: The Print Collector/Getty Images; 8 bottom left: Science & Society Picture Library/Getty Images; 10 bottom: The Picture Art Collection/Alamy Images; 12 inset top: Silver Screen Collection/Getty Images; 12 bottom right: John Springer Collection/Corbis/Getty Images; 13 top: Silver Screen Collection/Getty Images; 13 bottom: Lawrence Schiller/Polaris Communications/Getty Images; 15 top: Lt. J A Hampton/ Imperial War Museums via Getty Images; 16: Joe Petrella/NY Daily News Archive/Getty Images; 18 inset top: NASA Image Collection/Alamy Images; 18 bottom: Everett/Shutterstock; 21 top: NG Images/Alamy Stock Photo; 22 top: John Marton/The U.S. National Archive/GetArchive LLC; 24 top left: NASA; 26 inset top: Scott R. Kline; 28 bottom: Evening Standard/Hulton Archive/Getty Images; 29 bottom: Abbus Acastra/Alamy Stock Photo; 32 top: Dan Anderson/Elon University/Flickr; 34 top: Science History Images/Alamy Stock Photo; 35 top: Science History Images/Alamy Stock Photo; 36 top: National Inventors Hall of Fame; 36 bottom: DOE Photo/Alamy Stock Photo; 37 top: Adrian Cadiz/US Air Force/Wikimedia; 38 top: Glenn Research Center/NASA; 38 bottom: Bettina Flitner/laif/Redux; 39 top: Children's Climate Prize; 40 top left: Pictorial Press Ltd/Alamy Stock Photo; 40 top right: Bettmann/Getty Images; 40 bottom right: Universal Images Group North America LLC/Alamy Stock Photo; 42-43: pop_jop/Getty Images; 44 top: Niday Picture Library/Alamy Images; 44 bottom left: Scott R. Kline; 45 top: Silver Screen Collection/Getty Images; 45 center: NASA Image Collection/Alamy Images.

All other photos © Shutterstock.

10 9 8 7 6 5 4 3 2   150   23 24 25 26

Printed in the U.S.A. 113
First edition, 2022
Series produced for Scholastic by Parcel Yard Press

Contents

Super SHEroes Change the World

Women scientists, **engineers**, and inventors have made remarkable breakthroughs for centuries. Often, however, their achievements went unrecognized. Today far more women work in these fields than ever before, and their achievements are celebrated.

This book celebrates the life and the work of twelve of these women, twelve Super SHEroes of Science! They all worked, or still work, to advance **technology**.

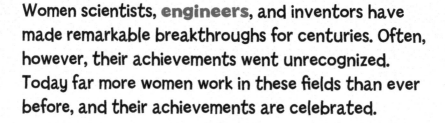

Technology uses science to improve or invent new devices or tools. Technology helps us make our lives easier.

SUPER SHEROES OF SCIENCE

Maanasa Mendu

Annie Easley

Gladys West

Hedy Lamarr

These Super SHEroes of Science changed the world in many different ways. They were involved in improving green energy, creating the Internet, helping build space rockets, and making computers better. And many of these women started off by being told that science wasn't for them. But they stuck to their dreams, asked questions, and took risks. They eventually got to write their own stories.

This book brings their stories to you! And while you read them, remember:

Your story can change the world, too! You can become a Super SHEro of Science.

Ada Lovelace

Ada was a computer **programmer** even before there were proper computers. She figured out how to write instructions that tell a machine to do a useful job. Today we call this coding.

SUPER SHERO OF SCIENCE

datafile

Born: 1815

Died: 1852

Place of birth: Great Britain

Role: Mathematician and Analyst

Super SHEro for: Inventing computer programming

Ada's family was very wealthy. Her mother encouraged Ada to have a curious mind and follow her interests. She saw that Ada loved math and science. She arranged for Ada to be schooled at home by the best teachers.

6

Ada's tour of Europe would have included Rome in what is now Italy.

When Ada was ten years old, she and her mother traveled around Europe for more than a year. Back in England, Ada spent hours looking at mechanical drawings and reading about new inventions. She designed her own steam-powered "flying carriage" when she was just twelve years old.

What's Your Story?

When designing her flying carriage, Ada studied the bodies of birds. She wanted to understand how they fly. She then wrote a book about flying machines called *Flyology*.

Have you ever studied animals in detail?

What animals did you choose?

Ada moved to London when she was seventeen years old.

Ada had the chance to meet many other wealthy people who had an interest in technology and science. When she was just seventeen years old, Ada met Charles Babbage, a mathematician and inventor.

Charles Babbage and his Difference Engine

Babbage had created a machine called the Difference Engine. His invention solved math problems like a modern calculator. Ada was fascinated by it. Babbage then designed an even more powerful machine called the Analytical Engine. It had a memory to hold numbers during long, complicated sums. That made the Analytical Engine the world's first computer. However, it was very complex and too expensive to build.

Did You Know?

An **algorithm** is a list of instructions that explains how to complete a task. It only works if you follow the steps in the correct order. The task could be anything, from controlling a computer game and steering a plane to doing the dishes. Try it yourself!

Step 1 Check the plate for dirt
       IF it is dirty go to Step 2
       IF it is clean go to Step 5
Step 2 Put the plate in soapy water
Step 3 Wipe the plate with a sponge
Step 4 Go to Step 1
Step 5 Dry the plate
Step 6 Put the plate away

This algorithm turns dirty dishes into clean ones.

ADA LOVELACE

Babbage asked Ada to rewrite a French report about his Analytical Engine into English. While Babbage thought his machine was a giant calculator, Ada had figured out that it could do more than just number calculations. She added her own ideas about it to the report. These extra notes were very important!

Ada included a set of instructions, or algorithm, on how to make the Analytical Engine do a complicated kind of math calculation. The Engine could do the calculation in minutes but it would take a person many days.

The world's first computer program, written by Ada Lovelace

Ada's instructions are the world's first computer program. She also suggested that the Analytical Engine could be programmed to work with letters, symbols, and music, like computers do today. **Ada's ideas inspired future computer scientists, and Ada Lovelace Day is held in October every year to celebrate all women scientists.**

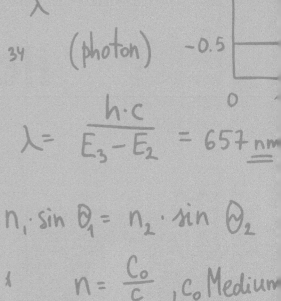

34 (photon)

$$\lambda = \frac{h \cdot c}{E_3 - E_2} = 657 \text{ nm}$$

$$n_1 \cdot \sin \Theta_1 = n_2 \cdot \sin \Theta_2$$

$$n = \frac{c_0}{c} , c_0 \text{ Medium}$$

$$\frac{\sin(45°)}{1,5} \Rightarrow$$

$$S = \dots \times 3mm = 0,5 \text{ m}$$

What Would You Do?

Without Ada's suggestions, Charles Babbage may not have realized what his machines could do. Teamwork can often achieve more.

What kind of work would you like to do as part of a team?

Is teamwork always the best way to get things done?

Hedy Lamarr

SUPER
SHEro
OF SCIENCE

Hedy Lamarr is best known as a Hollywood movie star. However, she was also a real-life inventor. Her radio system is now used in Wi-Fi.

Hedy was born in Vienna, Austria. Her real name was Hedwig Kiesler. She was always interested in technology. By the age of five, she had started to take apart her toys and then put them back together. She wanted to understand how everything worked.

datafile

Born: 1914

Died: 2000

Place of birth: Austria

Role: Actor and Inventor

Super SHEro for: Inventing a way to send radio signals that is now part of Wi-Fi systems

Hedy grew up in Austria.

A movie director in Berlin, Germany, offered Hedy acting classes when she was sixteen years old. Soon after, Hedy began acting in theaters and in small movies.

At just nineteen, Hedy got married to a businessman. However, she was very unhappy and left him, moving to the United States. Hedy found fame in Hollywood movies, but she kept her interest in inventions. She met Howard Hughes, a businessman who made movies and built aircraft. Hedy helped him design his airplane's wings so it would fly faster.

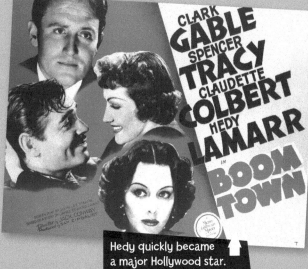

CLARK **GABLE**
SPENCER **TRACY**
CLAUDETTE **COLBERT**
HEDY **LAMARR**
IN
BOOM TOWN

Hedy quickly became a major Hollywood star.

Howard Hugh's plane, called the Spruce Goose flying boat, held the world record for the longest wings until 2019.

Even during her acting years, Hedy spent her spare time coming up with ideas. Her inventions included a better kind of traffic light and a fizzy tablet that mixed into water to create a soda drink.

Hedy wanted to help the United States and the **Allies** win World War II. Enemy submarines were sinking many ships. She thought better **torpedoes** could fight back against the submarines. Her musician friend George Antheil worked with her on this project.

What's Your Story?

? Hedy never stopped inventing. She combined her job as an actor with her passion as an inventor.

Would you follow your dreams, even if it didn't bring you fame or wealth?

Would you try to do both?

Torpedoes could be guided to their targets using radio signals. However, those signals could be blocked by the enemy. Hedy came up with a new system, where the torpedoes' radio signals would "hop" from **frequency** to frequency. If the signal kept changing like this, it could not be blocked, and the torpedo would find its target.

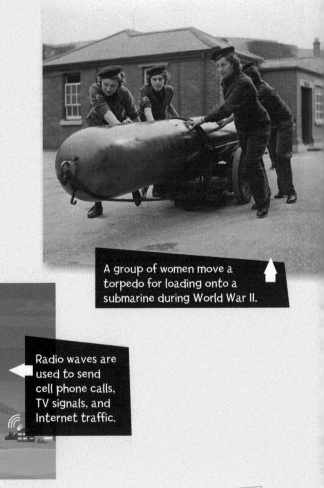

A group of women move a torpedo for loading onto a submarine during World War II.

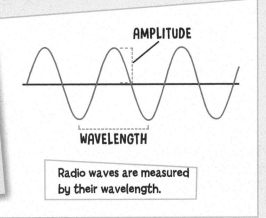

Radio waves are used to send cell phone calls, TV signals, and Internet traffic.

Did You Know?

A radio wave forms a rising and falling pattern, called a cycle. The distance a wave moves as it completes a cycle is its wavelength. The height of the wave is its amplitude. The number of cycles per second is called its frequency.

AMPLITUDE

WAVELENGTH

Radio waves are measured by their wavelength.

The two inventors were granted a **patent** in 1942. However, the US Navy said their system was too complicated. Instead, the military asked Hedy to help them as a celebrity. She put on shows for soldiers and helped raise money to pay for the army.

By the 1960s, the US Navy was using Hedy's "frequency-hopping" system to search for enemy submarines. Hedy and George never received any money for the use of their idea. Since then, their invention has become even more important.

Hedy used her fame to raise money for the US military.

Today, the frequency-hopping system is used by cell phones and in Wi-Fi networks. Without Hedy's innovations, the Internet would be very different!

Hedy was awarded the Electronic Frontier Foundation Pioneer Award in 1997. She died three years later. **Hedy's work as the "mother of Wi-Fi" led to her being included in the National Inventors Hall of Fame in 2014.**

What Would You Do?

Hedy spent most of her life without being recognized for her inventions. That did not stop her from trying to do more.

Which is most important to you, your achievements or being given praise?

How would you make sure your hard work gets recognized?

Annie Easley

Annie Easley was a computer scientist who worked for NASA. She helped build space rockets and worked on early electric cars. Her work inspired many women of color to get involved in science and technology.

Annie Easley was born in Birmingham, Alabama. She was raised by her mother, who told her daughter she could be anything she wanted, as long as she worked hard. Annie's first job was being a teacher.

datafile

Born: 1933

Died: 2011

Place of birth: United States

Field: Mathematics, Computer and Rocket Science

Super SHEro for: Working as a rocket scientist and researching clean energy

Annie worked to make sure that Black Americans could vote in her home state of Alabama.

Annie spoke up against discrimination. In those days in Alabama many Black people had to pass a writing and history test if they wanted to vote in elections. Annie helped members of her community prepare for the test.

In 1954, Annie saw a newspaper story about math experts, or human computers, working at the National Advisory Committee for Aeronautics (NACA). Annie applied to work there and was so good at math that she was given the job. She was one of only four Black people among more than 2,000 workers.

Annie worked at a NASA base in Ohio, which is now called the Glenn Research Center.

What's Your Story?

Annie found her way to NASA when she saw a story about an interesting job–a human computer.

Have you seen a job description that interests you?

Do you think you could do a job even if you don't have previous experience for it?

Soon after, NACA became part of NASA, America's new government agency that had the job of putting people into space. Annie's job was working with electronic computers to do complicated calculations. Annie became an expert in fuels and batteries. She wrote code that solved difficult problems about making and using electricity. This included renewable power sources, like solar and wind energy. Annie worked on early hybrid vehicles. Today's electric cars use some of her technology.

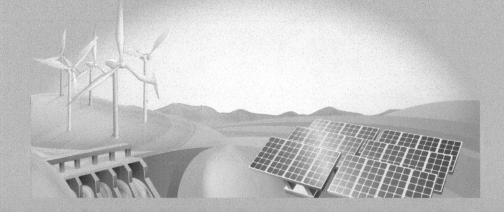

Next, Annie became a rocket scientist. She helped create the Centaur, a big rocket for launching heavy spacecraft. Annie would sometimes go to Cape Canaveral in Florida to watch the launches. Annie's work on the Centaur project was an important starting point for other big spacecraft, including the space shuttle.

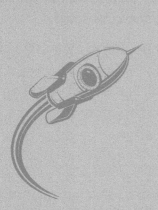

Some parts of the Centaur rocket were developed by Annie.

Did You Know?

A space rocket uses two liquid fuels called propellants. They are pumped into the combustion chamber at the bottom of the rocket. When mixed together, the liquids burn very hot and make a big rush of hot gas. As the gas blasts downward, it pushes the rocket upward. We have liftoff!

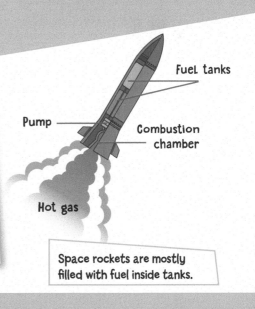

Fuel tanks

Pump

Combustion chamber

Hot gas

Space rockets are mostly filled with fuel inside tanks.

Annie was also an early pioneer of electric cars.

Annie was doing well at NASA, but things were not always fair or easy for her. For example, she was not paid as much as other coworkers. But she didn't let this affect her and was determined to improve things.

Almost twenty years after joining NASA, Annie went back to college to study mathematics. She was not given time off and had to work at NASA at the same time!

Later, Annie added a new role to her job at NASA by becoming a counselor. She helped out when staff said they were suffering discrimination.

Future space scientists will have a lot to thank Annie for.

Annie grew up at a time when there were few technology jobs for women, and there were even fewer for women of color. She wanted to address this unfairness whenever she could. **Annie will be remembered for many reasons. Her work for equal rights is as important as her research into computing, rocket science, and renewable energy.**

What Would You Do?

Annie faced many barriers to doing her job but she still managed to make a difference by working hard.

When have you used hard work to achieve your dreams?

What could you do to make life fairer for the future?

At Work with Annie Easley

Annie taught herself to be a computer and programming expert.

Annie was a natural at math. She didn't even need a college degree to get a job at NASA. Learn more about how she used her skills.

NASA

Annie started her career as a human computer. She would study complex problems and do calculations for researchers. Later, when electronic computers were in use, Annie's job title changed to "math technician." She learned how to program computers. Annie's programs showed engineers if their spacecraft and engine designs would work in real life.

Annie also used computers to study the damage being caused by **pollution** to the **ozone layer** high in Earth's **atmosphere**.

Annie faced discrimination. She had to pay for a university degree in math herself. Back then, NASA only paid college tuition for men!

During her time at NASA, she also had non-computing jobs. She mentored school kids and recruited new staff for NASA. Later in her career Annie became a work counselor. She would advise NASA leaders on how to solve problems of discrimination.

Annie at work

Primary role: Computer programming

Places of work: Offices and computer labs at NASA Glenn Research Center, Ohio

Daily activities: Research, complex math, computer programming, mentoring, and making the workplace fair

Main equipment: Computer, printer, pen, and paper

Computer

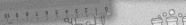

Pen and paper

Elizabeth Feinler

Elizabeth Feinler is an expert in managing information. She was among the first few people to work with what we now call the World Wide Web.

SUPER SHERO OF SCIENCE

Elizabeth Feinler was born in Wheeling, West Virginia, during the Great Depression. Nicknamed Jake, Elizabeth had an interest in science and nature. The library was one of Elizabeth's favorite places. She read all the science books. When she was done with the children's section, she was given special permission to read the adult ones.

datafile

Born: 1931

Place of birth: United States

Role: Information Scientist

Super SHEro for: Developing early versions of the Internet and World Wide Web

Elizabeth grew up on Wheeling Island in the Ohio River.

Elizabeth was very clever but could not afford college fees. She won a scholarship in Cincinnati, Ohio, but it did not pay for the first year so she could not start. Instead, Elizabeth entered a college close to home and had two jobs to pay for it. She often worked nights at the library.

What's Your Story?

Elizabeth was the first in her family to attend college. She had to struggle to get there.

Have you faced any problems in studying the subjects you wanted?

Elizabeth used her free time out of school to learn more about the subjects that interested her.

What subjects fascinate you? How could you find out more about them?

Before computers took over the job, information was stored on paper—a lot of paper! ➡

Elizabeth started a PhD in biochemistry at Purdue University. However, she decided to take a break to earn some money. In the end she never went back to college.

She got a job collecting information about the new substances being created by chemists. She recorded them in an index, or directory. It was a big job, and it was all done without any computers. Elizabeth then joined the Stanford Research Institute (SRI) in California. At SRI, Elizabeth started using computers to handle information.

Before the Internet, the fastest way to get information was by making a phone call. ➡

She became involved with the ARPANET, a new kind of computer network. Many years later this system became known as the Internet. The ARPANET was originally meant for use by the US military to communicate in safe ways, even during an enemy attack. However, the system could carry any kind of message, and universities and big companies started using it for sharing information.

The Internet started in 1969. This map shows where it was connected by 1984.

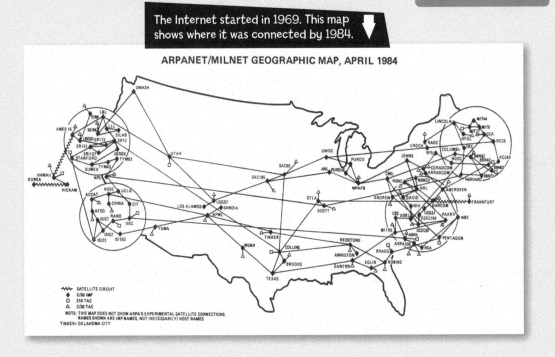

ARPANET/MILNET GEOGRAPHIC MAP, APRIL 1984

Elizabeth became an information scientist working for ARPANET. Her main job was to create a handbook, or user guide, to help people from all over the world work with the ARPANET systems.

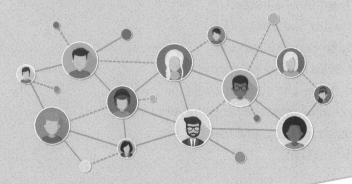

Did You Know?

The Internet is a system that connects the world's computers so they can share information. The sender's computer breaks up a message into small "packets." Each packet travels by itself through the Internet finding its way to the receiver's computer. The packets are then put back together to make the full message. If anything is missing, a request goes back to the start to send the packets again. Eventually the whole message will be received.

SENDER

Information travels through the Internet in little packets of data.

RECEIVER

She then set up the first WHOIS list, which is still working today. It records details about who owns every website. Elizabeth helped invent the domain naming system of .com, .edu, .gov, .mil, .org, and .net, which is still in use. Her team also designed a system for making it easier to use email.

Elizabeth helped make the Internet and the web what they are today. In 2012, she joined the Internet Hall of Fame.

Computer History Museum

Elizabeth volunteers at the Computer History Museum in California, helping explain the history of the Internet.

http://www.

What Would You Do?

Elizabeth wanted women engineers to have the same opportunities as male engineers. Elizabeth promoted women to be managers, and made sure they were all paid the same as the men.

If you were supervising a team, would you choose to have an equal number of men and women? If so, why?

At Work with Elizabeth Feinler

Elizabeth accepting an award

Elizabeth was interested in organizing information. Her ideas made the Internet easier for everyone to use. Find out how that happened.

Elizabeth's skill is gathering information together and recording it in a way that other people can use easily. To begin with, Elizabeth did all this work by writing and typing information onto paper. She then had printers publish the documents in books and catalogs for other people to search through.

Even when she began working on the ARPANET computer network, Elizabeth was still using paper documents. She headed a team of more than forty people. They kept information about the people who used the ARPANET and what they did. This system worked a bit like a Google search, except people had to call up with a question on the phone!

Record cards

Elizabeth at work

Elizabeth's team also managed the list of ARPANET's main computers, or servers. Anyone who wanted to add one would have to ask them for permission. The team was very busy, and Elizabeth sometimes worked through the night to keep up.

Elizabeth later moved to work at NASA and helped to set up its first websites.

Primary role: Managing information

Places of work: Library, office, and computer lab

Daily activities: Organizing information in an effective way

Main equipment: Record cards, telephone, computer

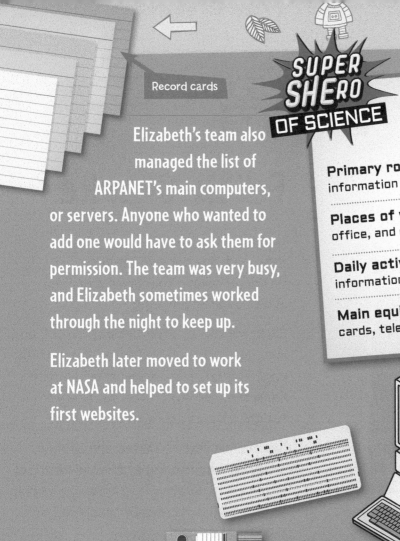

Early computer

Advancing **Technology** ELECTRICITY

Edith Clarke
(United States, 1883–1959)

Edith Clarke

Edith Clarke was raised on a farm in Maryland. She became the first American woman to receive a degree in electrical engineering.

Edith worked at General Electric (GE), and invented a device that made it easier for engineers to measure electricity in wires. Edith then moved to Turkey, where she taught physics at a women's college.

Back in the United States, she taught electrical engineering at the University of Texas. Edith was the first American woman to be a college professor teaching this important subject.

Grace Hopper

Grace Hopper was an early computer scientist. She joined the US Navy and worked at its computer department at Harvard University.

Grace helped develop IBM's Mark I, one of the first electronic computers. She also came up with the term "bug" to mean a programming error.

Grace and her team then created FLOW-MATIC, a programming language that used ordinary words as commands. This later became COBOL (Common Business-Oriented Language). Soon COBOL was the most popular programming language in the world. After her death, Grace was awarded the Presidential Medal of Freedom.

Grace Hopper
(United States, 1906-1992)

Erna Schneider Hoover

Advancing
Technology
TELEPHONES

Erna worked as a college professor before joining Bell Labs, a high-tech research center. She designed a computerized system for directing telephone calls. This was the first step in changing the telephone network from a mechanical system to a computerized one.

Erna Schneider Hoover
(United States, born 1926)

Advancing
Technology
NUCLEAR ENERGY

The Calutron Girls
(United States, 1945)

The Calutron Girls

At the height of World War II, thousands of young women worked at a secret government base in Tennessee. They operated machines called calutrons that produced very pure **uranium**. This was later used for making powerful atomic weapons. At the time, the Calutron Girls did not know how their work would be used.

Gladys West

Gladys West
(United States, born 1930)

Gladys West grew up in rural Virginia and studied math at college. She became one of just four Black people working at a US Navy lab in Dahlgren, Virginia, in 1956. Her job was doing complex calculations, first on paper, then by programming computers.

In 1978, Gladys began work on Seasat, a new satellite for observing the oceans. After that she was involved with Geosat, a satellite that mapped Earth's surface. Gladys's work was then used in the Global Positioning System (GPS), which uses satellites to show exactly where you are on Earth. GPS is used by navigation systems such as those used in cars and on smartphones.

SUPER
SHEROES
OF SCIENCE

Olga González-Sanabria

Advancing
Technology
SPACECRAFT

Olga González-Sanabria
(Puerto Rico, born 1950)

Olga was born in Puerto Rico, and she studied chemistry at university. She worked for NASA's Glenn Research Center for over thirty years, where she was the highest-ranking Hispanic employee. Olga was a key figure in creating the long-lasting batteries that are used to power the International Space Station. She won an award for this work.

Ursula Keller

Ursula is a physicist, inventor, and engineer. She is best known for using lasers to detect what substances are inside different materials. In 2005, her invention was considered for a Nobel Prize, the top science award. Ursula works in Zurich, Switzerland. She has set up a support network for other female researchers.

Advancing
Technology
LASERS

Ursula Keller
(Switzerland, born 1959)

Maanasa Mendu

As a child, Maanasa often visited her grandparents in India. She noticed how rural areas often suffered power outages. She decided to design an energy-gathering device called HARVEST. It uses three power sources—solar power, the wind, and rain— to make electricity. At just thirteen years old, Maanasa won the 2016 Young Scientist Challenge for her invention. She later developed LeafAI, an artificial intelligence system that can spot if crops have a disease. Maanasa continues to develop ideas, taking her inspiration from the natural world.

Maanasa Mendu
(United States, born 2003)

TimeLine

Here are some highlights in the history of advancing technology.

The Calutron Girls work producing very pure uranium. Without their knowledge, it is later used to create atomic weapons.

Hedy Lamarr is jointly granted a US patent for her frequency-hopping technology.

Computer language COBOL is developed based on Grace Hopper's FLOW-MATIC programming language.

ARPANET, an early version of the Internet, is turned on, connecting universities across the United States.

| 1843 | 1942 | 1943 | 1945 | 1947 | 1959 | 1960-1970 | 1969 |

Construction of the first programmable electronic computer, ENIAC, begins.

Edith Clarke joins the University of Texas, becoming the first female professor of electrical engineering in the country.

Annie Easley works on software for the Centaur rocket system.

Ada Lovelace's notes about using algorithms for the Analytical Engine are published.

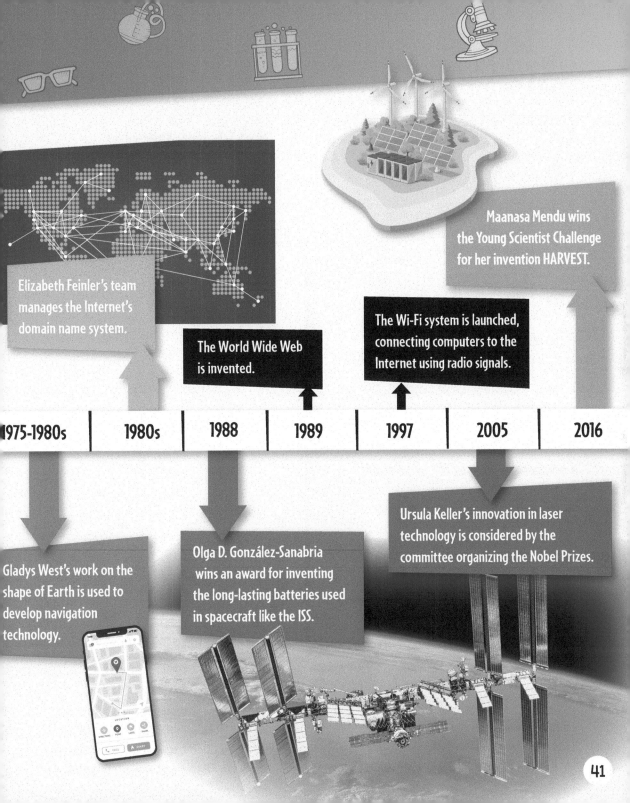

Elizabeth Feinler's team manages the Internet's domain name system.

Maanasa Mendu wins the Young Scientist Challenge for her invention HARVEST.

The World Wide Web is invented.

The Wi-Fi system is launched, connecting computers to the Internet using radio signals.

| 1975-1980s | 1980s | 1988 | 1989 | 1997 | 2005 | 2016 |

Ursula Keller's innovation in laser technology is considered by the committee organizing the Nobel Prizes.

Gladys West's work on the shape of Earth is used to develop navigation technology.

Olga D. González-Sanabria wins an award for inventing the long-lasting batteries used in spacecraft like the ISS.

41

SUPER SHEROES OF SCIENCE

Where in the World?

1. Calutron Girls
Oak Ridge, Tennessee
The Calutron Girls purified uranium at a secret government base in Tennessee during World War II.

2. Edith Clarke
Istanbul, Turkey
Edith Clarke taught physics at the Constantinople Women's College in Turkey.

3. Annie Easley
Cleveland, Ohio
Annie Easley worked at the NASA Glenn Research Center in Ohio, developing software for use in the Centaur rocket system.

4. Elizabeth Feinler
California
Elizabeth Feinler joined the Stanford Research Institute in Menlo Park, California, and worked on the early Internet.

5. Olga D. González-Sanabria
Cleveland, Ohio
Olga D. González-Sanabria became the highest-ranked Hispanic at NASA Glenn, working on batteries for spacecraft.

6. Erna Schneider Hoover
New Jersey
Working at Bell Labs in New Jersey, Erna Schneider Hoover began the computerization of the telephone network.

7. Grace Hopper
Cambridge, MA
Grace Hopper joined the Harvard Computation Lab in Massachusetts to work on IBM's early electronic computers.

North America

Atlantic Ocean

4. 9.   5.   3. 6. 7.   12.1.

Pacific Ocean

South America

N

8. Ursula Keller
Zurich, Switzerland
Inventor Ursula Keller develops a way of using lasers to scan for substances inside all kinds of materials.

10. Ada Lovelace
London, England
Ada Lovelace writes the world's first computer program for a new invention called the Analytical Engine in London, England.

11. Maanasa Mendu
Rural India
Seeing the many energy problems while visiting her grandparents in India, thirteen-year-old Maanasa Mendu invented a green-energy device, named HARVEST.

Arctic Ocean

10.

8.

2.

Europe

Asia

Pacific Ocean

11.

Africa

Indian Ocean

Australia

Southern Ocean

12. Gladys West
Dahlgren, Virginia
Gladys West began her career as a computer scientist working at a Navy lab in Virginia.

9. Hedy Lamarr
Hollywood, California
In between shooting Hollywood films, Hedy Lamarr helps to invent a new way of sending radio communications.

Words of Wisdom

Read the inspirational words of these Super SHEroes of Science and remember: You can become a Super SHEro, too!

Ada Lovelace

The more I study, the more insatiable do I feel my genius for it to be.

Grace Hopper

The only phrase I've ever disliked is, 'Why, we've always done it that way.' I always tell young people, 'Go ahead and do it [differently]. You can always apologize later.'

Elizabeth Feinler

The Internet completely changed the way people communicate and perform knowledge work, and the web has put the world's knowledge at everyone's fingertips.

Hedy Lamarr

66 The brains of people are more interesting than the looks I think. 99

Annie Easley

66 If I can't work with you, I will work around you. I was not about to be so discouraged that I'd walk away. 99

66 I had to be the best that I could be and always do things just right, to set an example for other people who were coming behind me, especially women. 99

Gladys West

66 There is no greater demand for women engineers, as such, as there is for women doctors; but there's always a demand for anyone who can do a good piece of work. 99

Edith Clarke

Glossary

algorithm (**al**-guh-*rith*-uhm) a list of instructions on how to do a certain job; used in computer programs

Allies (**al**-eyes) the countries that fought alongside the United States in World War II

atmosphere (**at**-muhs-*feer*) the layer of gases that surrounds Earth

discrimination (dis-*krim*-i-**nay**-shuhn) unfair behavior to others based on differences in such things as age, race, or gender

engineers (*en*-juh-**neerz**) people who use science to create useful structures and machines

frequency (**free**-kwuhn-see) the number of vibrations per second

Great Depression (grayt di-**presh**-uhn) a period when many people in the United States had no jobs

human computer (**hyoo**-muhn kuhm-**pyoo**-tur) a person who is very good at doing complex math

hybrid vehicle (**hye**-brid **vee**-i-kuhl) a car that has a gasoline engine and an electric motor

Nobel Prize (no-**bell** pryz) a top prize awarded for achievements in science, writing, and peacemaking

ozone layer (**oh**-zone **lay**-ur) a layer in the atmosphere that blocks out some of the sun's harmful rays

patent (**pat**-uhnt) a legal document giving the inventor the rights to make or sell it

physicist (**fiz**-i-sist) a person who studies the science of matter and energy, and of their relationship

pollution (puh-**loo**-shuhn) harmful materials that damage nature

programmer (**proh**-gram-ur) a person that writes the instructions that control a computer

renewable (ri-**noo**-uh-buhl) when something never runs out

technology (tek-**nah**-luh-jee) the use of science to do useful things

torpedo (tor-**pee**-doh) an underwater bomb shaped like a tube that targets ships and submarines

uranium (yu-**ray**-nee-uhm) an unstable metal that can explode

Index

Further Reading

Amson-Bradshaw, Georgia. *Pioneers of Science and Technology (Brilliant Women)*. New York: B.E.S, 2018

Brereton, Catherine. *Women Scientists in Math and Coding (Superwomen in STEM)*. Milwaukee, WI: Gareth Stevens Publishing, 2018

Lee Shetterly, Margot. *Hidden Figures: The True Story of Four Black Women and the Space Race*. New York: HarperCollins, 2018

Miller, J. P. *Groundbreaking Scientists (Black Stories Matter)* New York: B.E.S, 2020

Pierce, Nick. *Ada Lovelace (Women in Science)*. New York: Scholastic, 2019

About the Author

Supriya Sahai was born and raised in Delhi, India. She trained as a graphic designer and moved to the UK to pursue a master's degree. She has designed, illustrated, written, and published many books. But mostly she likes to sit down with a cup of coffee to read one. Supriya lives in Cambridge, England, with her family.

About the Consultant

Isabel Thomas is a science communicator and American Association for the Advancement of Science award-winning author. She has degrees in Human Sciences from the University of Oxford and in Education Research from the University of Cambridge, where her academic research focused on addressing inequalities in aspiration and access to science education and careers.